Contents

Cat

1 Start by drawing this shape for the head.

2 Add an ear, nose, eye, mouth and whiskers.

3 Draw in a bean-shaped body.

you can do it!

Use a felt-tip for the lines and add colour using coloured pencils.

4 Add two back legs and a belly shape.

Splat-a-fact

Cats sleep for 16-18 hours a day.

5 Draw in two front legs and a tail.

4

It's fun to draw
Pets

Mark Bergin

Author:

Mark Bergin was born in Hastings, England. He has illustrated an award winning series and written over twenty books. He has done many book designs, layouts and storyboards in many styles including cartoon for numerous books, posters and adverts. He lives in Bexhill-on-sea with his wife and three children.

Editorial Assistant:

Victoria England

HOW TO USE THIS BOOK:

Start by following the numbered splats on the left hand page. These steps will ask you to add some lines to your drawing. The new lines are always drawn in red so you can see how the drawing builds from step to step. Read the 'You can do it!' splats to learn about drawing and shading techniques you can use.

Published in Great Britain in MMXII by
Book House, an imprint of
The Salariya Book Company Ltd
25 Marlborough Place, Brighton BN1 1UB
www.salariya.com
www.book-house.co.uk

ISBN-13: 978-1-908177-57-5

1 3 5 7 9 8 6 4 2

A CIP catalogue record for this book is available
from the British Library.

Printed and bound in China.

PAPER FROM
SUSTAINABLE
FORESTS

Visit our website at **www.book-house.co.uk**
or go to **www.salariya.com** for **free** electronic versions of:
You Wouldn't Want to be an Egyptian Mummy!
You Wouldn't Want to be a Roman Gladiator!
You Wouldn't Want to be a Polar Explorer!
You Wouldn't Want to Sail on a 19th-Century Whaling Ship!

Visit our Bookhouse 100 channel to see Mark Bergin doing step
by step illustrations:

www.youtube.com/user/BookHouse100

Dog

1 Start with an oval for the head. Add cheeks and eyes.

2 Draw in the ears and add a bone in the dog's mouth.

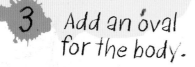

you can do it!

Use wax crayons to add colour and a felt-tip for the lines.

3 Add an oval for the body.

4 Draw in the back legs and the tail.

Splat-a-fact

Dogs have better hearing than humans and can hear sounds at four times the distance.

5 Draw in the front legs and add a collar.

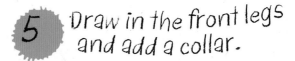

Fish

1 Start by drawing the body shape.

splat-a-fact

Fish sleep with their eyes open!

2

Add a curved line for the face. Draw in the mouth and a dot for the eye.

3 Add a tail and two fins.

4 Draw in the stripey markings.

8

9

Budgerigar

 **1** Start with the head. Add a beak and a dot for the eye.

2 Add a body and two feet.

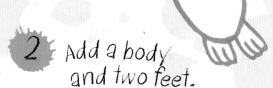

3 Draw in the tail feathers.

4

Add the wings.

you can do it!

Use oil pastels and smudge them with your finger. Use a felt-tip for the lines.

Guinea pig

you can do it!

Cut out the shapes from coloured paper and glue in place. The guinea pig head must overlap the body. Use felt-tip for the lines.

1 Start by cutting out a curvy shape for the body. Stick it down.

2 Cut out the head shape with tufts of hair. Stick down.

4 Cut out four feet and brown fur for the guinea pig's back. Stick down.

3 Cut out a brown patch for the face. Stick it down. Cut out an ear and stick down. Draw in the eye and nose.

Splat-a-fact

A group of guinea pigs is called a herd.

MAKE SURE YOU GET AN ADULT TO HELP YOU WHEN USING SCISSORS!

13

Horse

you can do it!

Use wax crayons to create various textures. Paint over with watercolour paint. Use a felt-tip for the lines.

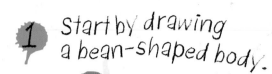

1 Start by drawing a bean-shaped body.

2 Draw in a neck and a head. Add dots for eyes and nostrils.

3 Draw in four legs with hooves.

Splat-a-fact

Male foals are called colts and female foals are called fillies.

4 Add a tail and a mane. Draw in ears and spots on the body. Add a piece of grass to the mouth.

Lizard

1 Start with this shape for the head.

2 Add two circles with dots for the eyes, a mouth and dots for the nostrils.

you can do it!

Use a felt pen for the lines then paint with watercolour. Add coloured inks to the wet paint for interest.

3 Draw in a wiggly body shape.

4 Add legs and splayed feet. Draw in markings on the body.

16

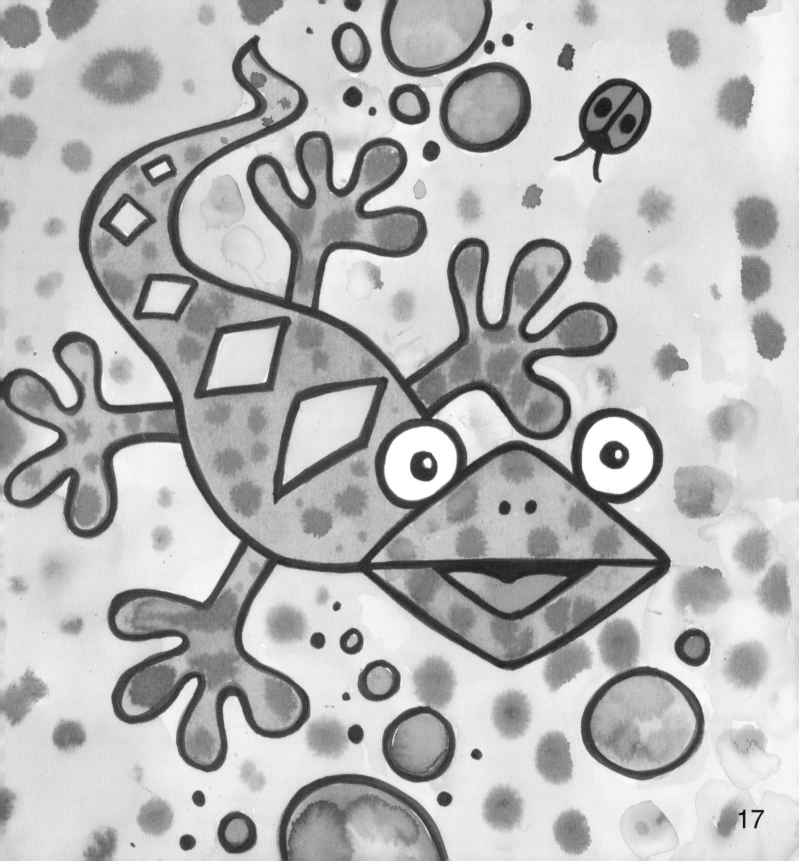

Parrot

1 Start by drawing the head shape. Add a dot for the eye.

2 Add the body and the beak.

3 Draw in the wings and tail feathers.

4 Add the feet and perch.

5 Draw in the feathers.

you can do it!

Add colour with watercolour paint. Use felt-tips for the lines.

Rabbit

Splat-a-fact

Rabbits can run about 35 miles an hour.

1 Start by drawing a circle for the head.

2 Add ears.

you can do it!

Use oil pastels and smudge them with your finger. Use a felt-tip for the lines.

3 Draw in the eyes, nose, mouth, teeth and whiskers.

4 Add a rounded body and two back feet.

5 Draw in the front legs and paws.

Rat

1 Start with the head shape. Add a dot for the eye.

2 Draw in two ears, a nose, mouth and whiskers.

3 Draw in the body.

4 Draw in the two back legs.

5 Draw in the front legs, and a tail. Add toes to each foot.

You can do it!
Draw the lines with a felt-tip and then add colour with watercolour paint.

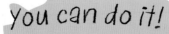

Snake

1 Start by drawing this head shape.

2 Add dots for the eyes and nostrils.

splat-a-fact
Snakes belong to the animal group called reptiles.

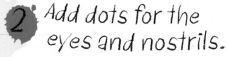

3 Draw in the mouth and add a forked tongue.

4 Draw a long, curving body.

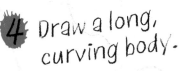

you can do it!
Draw the lines with a felt-tip and use torn tissue paper for colour.

5 Add a diamond shaped pattern.

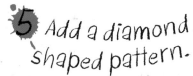

stick insect

1 Start with the head shape. Add dots for eyes.

2 Add two antennae and pincer shapes under the head.

3 Draw in the stick insect's body.

splat-a-fact
Stick insect eggs can take up to 2 years to hatch.

4 Add three legs and feet to each side.

spider

1 Start by drawing two overlapping circles for the head and body.

splat-a-fact

Spiders have eight legs and two body parts, the abdomen and the thorax.

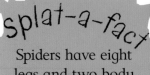

2 Add four dots for the eyes and two fangs.

3 Draw in three legs on each side.

you can do it!
Colour the picture with wax crayons. First place different textured surfaces under the paper to create interesting effects.

4 Add two more front legs.

28

Tortoise

you can do it!
Colour in with watercolour paint. Use a felt-tip for the lines.

1 Start with an oval shape for the shell.

2 Add pattern to the shell. Draw in another curved line around the shell's base.

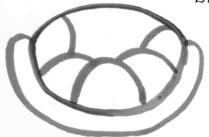

3 Draw in the head and add an eye, mouth and nostrils.

4 Add four legs and a pointed tail.

Splat-a-fact
Tortoises have a protective shell around their bodies.

30

Index

Download our free iPhone and
iPad catalogue app. Search for
Salariya or Book House

www.salariya.com
where books come to life!

Follow us on Facebook
and Twitter

www.youtube.com/user/BookHouse100

Children's non-fiction and graphic novels

fiction

Fiction for children and teenagers

Free activities,
puzzles and web
books, with
information about
our books for
babies, toddlers
and pre-school

Four free web books

The Book House blog –
competitions, giveaways
and current news